be more Stitch

Be more **positive**, **happy**, and **confident** every day.

Written by Laura Gilbert
and Ellen Philpott

CONTENTS

FIND WHERE YOU FIT 4
- 'Ohana 6
- Find your people 8
- Make a memory book 10
- See the whole picture 12
- Would you rather...? 14

YOU DO YOU 16
- Discover your true self – and own it! 18
- Who are you? 20
- You don't need to blend in 22
- Things don't always go to plan 24

ALL THE FEELS 26
- Everybody gets cranky 28
- We can all be annoying! 30
- My journal 32
- Channel your energy 34
- Start again 36
- Have a great day! 38

FIND YOUR HAPPY 40
- Turn your feelings around 42
- Your happy might not be someone else's 44
- What do you love to do? 46
- Aaaand... relax! 48

FRIENDSHIP 50
- Some won't see the real you 52
- ... but others will 54
- How well do you know me? 56
- Keep being you 58
- Get a cheerleader 60

GLOSSARY 62

NICE TO MEET YOU!

You know when you make a new friend, you want to know everything about them – their name, their favourite movie, what makes them happy? Well, with *Be More Stitch*, you're going to make a brand-new friend – YOU!

There's no better time to start learning about who you are, just like Experiment 626, or Stitch as he's better known, does. Because when you do that, you'll be able to find your people, discover what makes you happy, and make really good friends.

So, hop on your surfboard – there are lots of big waves ahead!

FIND WHERE YOU FIT

Not many people think Stitch fits in. He doesn't. But finding where you *fit* is not about *fitting in*. It's about discovering those people that get you, those friends who will sing to you while you kick back with a coconut.

'OHANA

There are some people in your life who will always be there for you.

They might look different from you and might not speak the same language.

But even though they don't understand what you're saying, they **understand you**. They're the ones you want to enjoy a shave ice with. **Hold on to them –** they're your *'ohana*.

"*'Ohana* means family. Family means nobody gets left behind... or forgotten."

–Lilo and Nani

FIND YOUR PEOPLE

You'll have friends, family, and people you haven't met yet who feel like your people.

None of these relationships will be perfect though. Sometimes **your friends will be a pain**. And sometimes they'll think you're stinky!

But if they're *really your people*, then it'll work out and you can surf life's ups and downs together.

If you are having trouble with a friendship, follow this chart to help you decide what to do.

Do you feel good when you are with this person?

- **No**, they make me feel sad or angry.
- **Yes**, they are cute and fluffy! → Great. Share a coconut cake with them!

Have you tried telling them what is bothering you?

- **Yes** → Did they listen and try to change the thing that upset you?
  - **Yes**, they tried but they still don't get it. → Give them another chance – but don't let them be unkind to you.
- **No**, I don't think they would understand. → Talk to them and be clear about what is bothering you – maybe you can work things out.
- **No** → Try not to hang out with this person so much. Instead, spend time with people who appreciate you for you!

MAKE A MEMORY BOOK

Stitch doesn't have memories of what happened before he arrived on Earth. But since meeting his friend Lilo, he's made lots of them. And Lilo knows just the way to make sure those memories are not forgotten. Why not make a memory book to capture your favourite moments?

Give each page a theme by adding drawings.

"This is a great home. You'll like it a lot."

Add in special words that mean something to you.

Make your book colourful with washi tape.

You might want to show important events, like a birthday party, or just fun times with friends.

Don't forget to add a description for each picture.

SEE THE WHOLE PICTURE

Grown-ups don't get it! Just ask Lilo. No matter how you try to explain or **how loud you scream**, they don't always understand.

But give them a chance. They might start to see why that jar of peanut butter is so important to you, and show that – truly – they *still get you* and who you are.

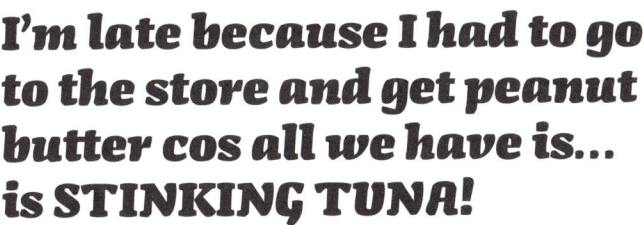

WOULD YOU RATHER...?

Play this "would you rather" game with a friend to get to know each other better.

Would you rather:

Be a **scientist** or an **artist**?

Be **poor and famous** or **rich and unknown**?

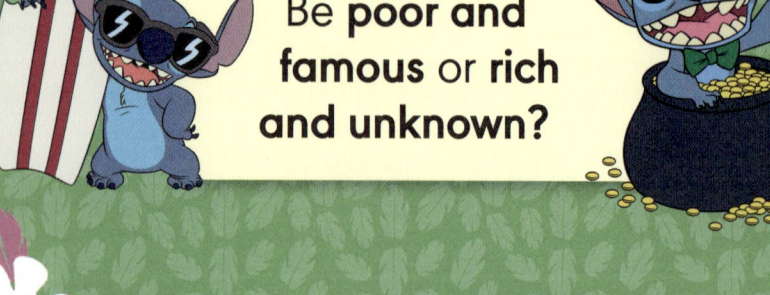

Go to **school** or do **hula dancing?**

Eat only **sandwiches all day** or eat only **fruit all day?**

Go to **space with Stitch** or go **surfing with David?**

Be able to **fly** or **turn invisible?**

YOU DO YOU

It's easy to follow the crowd and blend in. But if you're too scared to show the real record-playing Weirdlo that you are, then you'll likely feel blue. Be proud! After all, there's only one Experiment 626 – and only one you.

DISCOVER YOUR TRUE SELF – AND OWN IT!

We are all **lots of things** at once. Nani is a strict but caring big sister. Jumba is an evil genius but also easily persuaded.

However, there's always something deep inside you that is truly, uniquely you. That never changes. For Stitch, that's being fluffy! **Find your fluffy** and don't let anyone change it.

"I like fluffy."

—Stitch

What's your fluffy? Write it down or draw a picture of how it makes you feel.

WHO ARE YOU?

There's only one you in the entire universe. But you might have more in common with some people (or aliens) than you think.

How would you describe yourself?
A) Mischievous and fluffy
B) Caring, creative... and different
C) Hard worker and master of disguise. Can panic... sometimes... OK... all the time
D) Professional genius

It's the weekend! What will you be doing?
A) Baking a cake, playing guitar, surfing (without getting too wet)
B) Hula dancing
C) Weekend? What weekend? I live to work
D) Thinking up a new scientific experiment

What kind of friend are you?
A) As loyal as a puppy
B) I'm a friend for life
C) I rely on others
D) I'm easily persuaded on important matters

4 You're at a restaurant. What do you order?

A) Coconut cake washed down with coffee
B) Something from each of the four food groups
C) Pineapple shrimp (hold the mosquitoes)
D) Chicken drumsticks with coconut milk to drink

Mostly *B*s: You're most like **Lilo**

You like the things you like and some people don't understand that.

But stay true to yourself and your friends will love you for it.

Mostly *A*s: You're most like **Stitch**

You're one of a kind! There's no one quite like you. And to your buddies, you're a true friend.

Mostly *C*s: You're most like **Pleakley**

You like to follow the rules—and there's nothing wrong with that.

You tend to worry about things but, deep down, you know everything will be OK.

Mostly *D*s: You're most like **Jumba**

You know what you're good at and like to take charge.

But you can also see the other person's (or alien's) point of view.

YOU DON'T NEED TO BLEND IN

Want to know a secret? Come closer.
   Everyone's a Weirdlo.

There's no point hiding it or trying to blend in, even if you think it will protect you. You'll only make yourself feel blue. Be the weird and **_wonderful person_** you truly are, six arms and all. And your friends will enjoy your six-armed hug!

Find each of the characters listed below in this picture.

- ⭐ **Jumba**
- ⭐ **Pleakley**
- ⭐ **Lilo**
- ⭐ **Stitch in disguise**
- ⭐ **Sunbathing Stitch**
- ⭐ **Six-armed Stitch**

THINGS DON'T ALWAYS GO TO PLAN

So, you're going to get a dog – or an ice cream. What if that pup runs away or the scoop falls off the cone?

ALL YOUR PLANS ARE RUINED!!!

But **change can be a good thing**. The unexpected can lead you to something even better. If you're uptight about things, like Pleakley, you might miss the best part.

"Sometimes you try your hardest, but things don't work out the way you want them to. Sometimes things have to change. And maybe sometimes they're for the better."

—Nani

ALL THE FEELS

Feelings can be BIG! They can seem like they'll last forever and that nobody understands what you're going through.

Everyone has their good days and everyone has their bad days.
So, go where the waves take you.

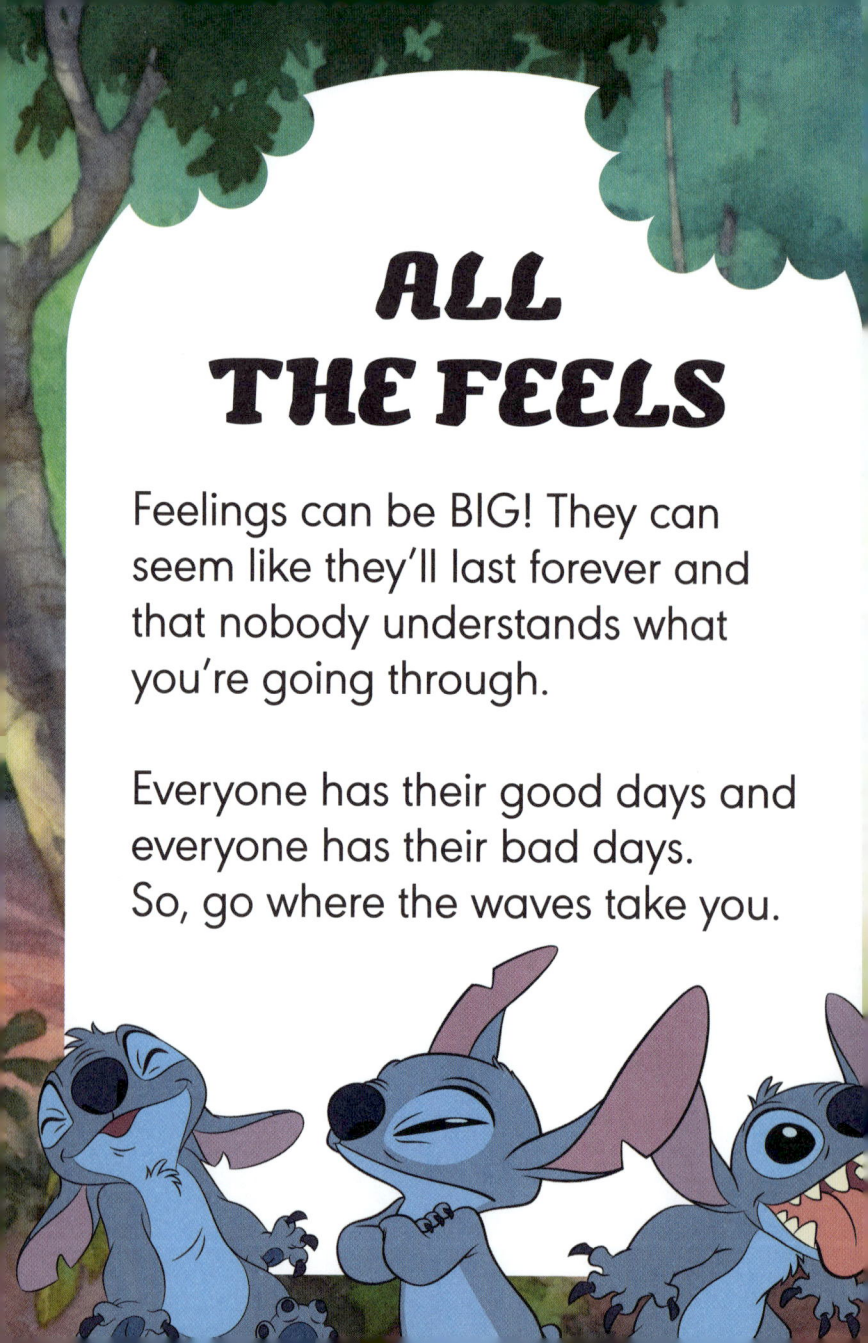

EVERYBODY GETS CRANKY

It's bedtime. **SULK!** Everyone thinks you're **just irritable**. But actually you want to finish that book or spend time with your grown-up.

Yes, you're cranky, but it means you're **feeling something else**. Can you explain those feelings to someone? Because you can bet your last plate of poi they'll know what it's like to feel that way.

Rainbow breaths can help you feel less cranky.

1 Make sure you are sitting comfortably. Stretch your arms out at your sides.

2 Imagine that your fingers are marker pens and you are going to draw a rainbow in the sky above you.

3 Breathe in slowly and at the same time, lift your arms up, drawing an arch in the air over you like a rainbow.

4 Touch your hands together at the top, and then, as you breathe out, bring them back down to your sides.

5 Do this five times, nice and slowly.

"He's just cranky because it's his bedtime."

—Lilo

WE CAN ALL BE ANNOYING!

AAAAAAH!!!

People can be *really* **annoying!** Like scream into your pillow annoying. But, want to know something? You can be annoying, too!

AAAAAH!!!

Think about when you and a friend got annoyed at each other. Can you see their side of things?

So next time you're getting frustrated, try thinking of what the other person might be feeling. There are **two sides** to every story.

MY JOURNAL

A lot can happen in a day. Just ask Stitch. One moment, he's in outer space, the next his home is a dog shelter! And a lot of feelings can be felt in a day, too. It can help you to make sense of them by writing or drawing in your own journal.

1

Pick a notebook. Do you want the cover to be your favourite colour? Are you going to decorate it? Do you want the book to have a lock on it? Do you want lined pages or plain?

2

Take 5-10 minutes near the end of each day to write down or draw some of the things you've done or felt that day. Use the prompts on the next page to help you.

3 After you've been keeping your journal for a little while, look back on your entries. Do you feel different about some of those events now? Are the feelings as strong as they were when you wrote them down?

Write about or draw something fun you did today.

Write about something that didn't go well today. What would you have preferred to happen?

Make a list of a few things that were really good about today.

What are you looking forward to tomorrow and why?

CHANNEL YOUR ENERGY

Ever get so excited or annoyed or worried that you *feel you're about to burst?*

You've got all this energy inside you, just like Stitch. He doesn't mean to ruin Lilo's room or get milkshake everywhere.

Try putting that **energy** somewhere else by drawing or kicking a ball or dancing or making a model of San Francisco, for instance!

"Why not try and make something for a change?"
— Lilo

Imagine being Stitch and then see if you can focus that energy!
Set a timer and count how many of these you can do in one minute.

- Star jumps
- Burpees
- Lunges
- Squats

Then do it again tomorrow and see if you can beat your own score!

START AGAIN

Lilo and Nani know what it's like when you have days where **nothing goes right**. You fight and fall out and if you can make up before the sun sets then that's amazing!

But tomorrow is always a ***new day*** and a new chance to start again, whatever has happened the day before.

HAVE A GREAT DAY!

What would make a great day for you?
Choose one from each of these options.

Shave ice *or* **coconut cake?**

Sunshine *or* **snow?**

New adventures *or* **relaxing?**

Red outfit *or* **yellow outfit?**

Hula dancing *or* **surfing?**

FIND YOUR HAPPY

You can't be happy all the time. But when you know what cheers you up or chills you out, then you can help get a bit of your happy back. Maybe, like Stitch, listening to your top tunes is guaranteed to put a smile on your face. Whatever your happy is, and no matter what anyone else thinks, embrace it!

TURN YOUR FEELINGS AROUND

When you're feeling blue (not blue like Stitch, but sad blue) or worried, you can sometimes *change that feeling*.

Think of something you love doing, whether it's **surfing** the waves, **dancing** to your favourite songs, or, in Stitch's case, eating **dessert** – and do it!

Just a change of outlook can help.

What activity always makes you feel happy?

"Stitch is troubled. He needs desserts!"

—Lilo

YOUR HAPPY MIGHT NOT BE SOMEONE ELSE'S

Stitch can think of nothing worse than surfing in the ocean, but, for David, that's his ***favourite place*** to be.

Once you've discovered your **happy place** or **special hobby**, look at what floats other people's boats (or surfboards).

You never know – you might find a new passion.

"I might not be a doctor, but I know there's no better cure for a sour face than a couple of boards and some choice waves."

—David

WHAT DO YOU LOVE TO DO?

Answer the following questions about your interests:
If you answer mostly **blue**, you would enjoy a creative hobby – you could play the guitar like 𝒮𝓉𝒾𝓉𝒸𝒽!
If you answer mostly **orange**, you might enjoy a new sport, like 𝒟𝒶𝓋𝒾𝒹.
If you answer mostly **yellow**, you like being with friends and family, just like ℒ𝒾𝓁ℴ.
If you answer mostly **pink**, you might love science and inventing, like 𝒥𝓊𝓂𝒷𝒶.

Where would you rather go on holiday?

A beach in Hawaii	Camping with family
A crafting course	A science workshop

What would you most like to be when you grow up?

Inventor	Poet or writer
YouTuber	Olympic athlete

What would be your dream birthday gift?

- A guitar and microphone
- A surfboard or other sports equipment
- A cool phone to message your friends
- A chemistry set

If you could learn a new skill in a day, what would you choose?

- Robotics
- Learning a language
- Snowboarding
- Photography

How would you prefer to spend the day?

- At home with family
- In an art gallery
- In a science lab
- At the sports centre

What would be your favourite outfit?

- Comfy clothes you can run around in
- Something you've designed yourself
- A T-shirt with an arty print
- The same as your best friend!

AAAAND... RELAX!

Has your grown-up ever said to you "Just breathe!" or "Take a breath?" It might sound weird, but breathing and being aware of your breathing can help you calm down or slow down.

1 Lie down in a comfortable spot and close your eyes. Relax your arms and legs.

2 Put a soft toy, like Scrump, on your belly and watch it move as you breathe in and out slowly.

3 Breathe in and, as you breathe out, make a whooshing sound like the sound of the ocean waves.

How do you feel now?
How does your body feel?
What are you thinking?

FRIENDSHIP

Having true friends is one of life's real joys, whether you have one or twenty-one! While you can't be friends with everyone, riding life's highways with a real buddy is just the best. And *being* a good friend is really quite cool, too!

SOME WON'T SEE THE REAL YOU...

Here's a tough **life lesson**: You can't be everybody's friend. There. We've said it.

Some people may not like you. You may not like them. They **might see you differently** from how you truly are. Or you might not have anything in common.

That's OK.
Your friends are out there. And they're worth the wait.

Look at the different qualities below and decide whether they are ones you want in a friend or not.

- Bosses me around
- Keeps my secrets
- Makes me laugh
- Makes fun of me
- Only plays with me if there's no one else around
- Says kind words
- Helps me when I have a problem
- Calls me names
- Enjoys the same things as me
- Doesn't share

... BUT OTHERS WILL

To some folk, Stitch is a **little monster**, but to Lilo he's her **little angel**. Lilo sees the true Stitch underneath all the mischief!

Find friends that smile at you the way Lilo smiles at Stitch – they're the ones who see the *real you!*

Tell a friend what you like best about them.

"Yes. He's good. I can tell."

—Lilo

HOW WELL DO YOU KNOW ME?

Grab a friend or member of your family and see how many questions about you they can get right. Once you're done, swap over and answer the same questions about them.

1 What's my favourite colour?

2 Do I prefer the sunshine or the snow?

3 Who is my best friend?

4 What chore do I hate doing?

5 Do I have a nickname? What is it?

6 What's my favourite movie?

7 Do I like dogs best or cats? Or neither?

8 Would I ever want to go into space?

Talk about which questions you got right and which you didn't.

KEEP BEING YOU

Mertle Edmonds doesn't understand Lilo.
And **that's hard** when you want to be friends with someone.

But whatever you do, ***don't change yourself*** to fit in. You're your own unique specialness. Just because someone doesn't know what to say to you doesn't mean there's something wrong with you.

"People treat me different."

—Lilo

Think about all the things that make you you.

"They just don't know what to say."

—Nani

Look around your house and garden or nearby outside space. Find 10 small things that say something about you. It could be a note from a friend, a shell, a toy, a photo, or anything that is special to you. Find a shoebox or container to put them in. Then decorate the treasure box.

GET A CHEERLEADER

As you travel along your path, you'll meet those who will put you down or tell you you can't do something. **Don't listen** to those folks.

Just like Stitch has Lilo, find the people who *build you up*. Those who tell you you *can* do it!

They're your own little cheer team, your *'ohana*.

GLOSSARY

appreciate
like or value something or someone

channel your energy
when you take the energy you have and focus it on one thing

embrace
accept something completely and enjoy it

irritable
easily annoyed

journal
a book you write in about your day and your feelings

'ohana
Hawaiian word for "family"

passion
something you have a strong interest in

poi
a Hawaiian savoury dish made from mashed taro root, a root vegetable

qualities
features or characteristics of someone

shave ice
a dessert of ice shavings flavoured with syrup, popular in Hawaii

washi tape
a sticky tape, often with pictures on, used in crafts

Weirdlo
the nickname Mertle Edmonds gives Lilo to indicate Lilo is weird – in *her* opinion!

Written by Laura Gilbert and Ellen Philpott
Designer Callum Midson
Cover design Nic Davies
Art Director Charlotte Coulais
Senior Production Editor Jennifer Murray
Production Controller Laura Andrews
Senior Managing Editor Rachel Lawrence
Managing Director Mark Searle

First published in Great Britain in 2025
by Dorling Kindersley Limited
20 Vauxhall Bridge Road,
London SW1V 2SA

The authorised representative in the EEA is
Dorling Kindersley Verlag GmbH. Arnulfstr. 124,
80636 Munich, Germany

Page design copyright © 2025 Dorling Kindersley Limited
A Penguin Random House Company
10 9 8 7 6 5 4 3 2 1
004–348366–May/2025

© Disney 2025

All rights reserved.
No part of this publication may be reproduced, stored in or introduced into a retrieval system, or transmitted, in any form, or by any means (electronic, mechanical, photocopying, recording, or otherwise), without the prior written permission of the copyright owner.

No part of this publication may be used or reproduced in any manner for the purpose of training artificial intelligence technologies or systems. In accordance with Article 4③ of the DSM Directive 2019/790, DK expressly reserves this work from the text and data mining exception.

A CIP catalogue record for this book
is available from the British Library.
ISBN 978-0-2417-2816-1

Printed and bound in Slovakia

www.dk.com

MIX
Paper | Supporting
responsible forestry
FSC™ C018179

This book was made with Forest Stewardship Council™ certified paper – one small step in DK's commitment to a sustainable future.
Learn more at www.dk.com/uk/information/sustainability